BIBLE VISUALS international

Helping Children See Jesus

ISBN: 978-1-64104-134-8

The Life and Death of DAVID BRAINERD

Author: Joseph Tyrpak
Illustrators/Computer Graphic Artists: Bethany and Olivia Moy
Page Layout: Patricia Pope

© 2020 Bible Visuals International
PO Box 153, Akron, PA 17501-0153
Phone: (717) 859-1131
www.biblevisuals.org

For other formats of this story and related items, please visit www.biblevisuals.org and search using the title or the item "5271".

Chapter 1
Childhood and Conversion

My name is David Brainerd. I lived in America three hundred years ago, and God gave me just 29 years of life. (David lived from April 1718 to October 1747.) In those few years He gave me, I enjoyed many, many sweet days—many days when I saw God working in me and many days when I saw Him working through me. But God allowed my life to be filled with deep sadness, too. Today I want to tell you about a few of the saddest times in my childhood along with one of the happiest days of my life. Here's how I'm going to do it: I'm going to tell you about two very sad times, then about the one really happy day.

Here's the first sad experience I want to tell you about: both of my parents died before I turned fourteen. My family lived in Haddam [(pronounced HAT-um), Connecticut.

I grew up in a large house that sat on a very large property right next to the Connecticut River. Our house needed to be large because I was the sixth of nine children. Yes, you heard me correctly: I had eight siblings – four sisters and four brothers! Our house sat up on a hill in Haddam and overlooked the beautiful, wide river that flows calmly most of the year. My father (his name was Hezekiah) was a very important politician in the British colony of Connecticut. (Remember, I lived in this country when we were still colonies of England – before this country was ever called "The United States of America.") When I was nine years old, my father became sick and died. And just a few years later, when I was 13, my mother, Dorothy, came down with a sickness that was going around Haddam, and she died, too. When I was growing up, it was much more dangerous to get sick than it is today. In those days, there weren't as many doctors or medicines as there are now. And when I grew up, it was common for people to get sick with some unknown disease and die. The year after my mom died, a deadly disease spread very quickly through my whole town. I had to leave my house and moved in with relatives who lived on the other side of the river.

I can't describe to you how sad it was for me to lose both my parents. During those years I cried a lot and I was always afraid of dying. (When reflecting on the death of his mother the exact words that David wrote in his diary were: "I was exceedingly distressed and melancholy....") But I can also tell you that I didn't give up. I kept going. There are times when life can get so sad that we're tempted to give up, but as I got older, I came to understand that God is in control of everything that happens. I've also come to learn that God is always good. God gives life, and God takes life, and life—no matter how hard it gets—is a precious and undeserved gift that God has given each of us. I don't know why God allowed my parents to die when I was so young, and I don't know why He allowed me to experience such deep sadness, but as I got older God gave me many happy days, too.

Before I share a really happy experience with you, I will tell you about another sad part of my childhood: Even though I grew up learning about the Bible and going to church every week, I didn't actually become a Christian until after I was 20-years old. I was 21 when I trusted Jesus to be my Saviour.

Throughout my childhood and teenage years, I was taught a lot about God, and much of what I heard I really didn't like. It bothered me that God didn't think I was a good person – I used to do a lot of good things like read my Bible and pray. But Bible teachers told me often that in God's eyes I was a sinner who couldn't do anything to make God like me and accept me. That bothered me. It also really annoyed me that God declared me to be a sinner for something that the first man Adam did. I didn't even have a choice about whether I was a sinner or not. It also really bothered me that God's rules were so strict, that even one act of disobedience made me guilty, and that God had only made one way for sinners to be rescued. All those things bothered me as I was growing up. I didn't think that God was generous and kind. To me He sounded mean, unfair, and strict. At one point I remember even saying that I wanted to get rid of God. (Brainerd actually said, "I longed to pull the eternal God out of His throne and stamp Him under my feet.")

So now I've told you two very sad things about me – about how my parents died when I was little and how, as I grew up, I really didn't like the God that I was learning about. But now I want to tell you about one of the happiest days of my life – about how God changed my heart. Throughout my childhood I continued to go to church in Haddam, and I kept learning about the Bible, even though I didn't like all of it. As I got older someone recommended that I read a little book that was written by a very famous pastor named Solomon Stoddard. The book was called *A Guide to Christ*. As I read that book, I learned that many people, before they become Christian, think of themselves as pretty good – certainly not bad enough to go to hell. I learned that many people get angry with God when they realize they can't do anything by themselves to earn God's forgiveness. Before I read this helpful little book, I didn't realize that many people thought the same way I did. God used that little book to show me that I needed to be saved and how I could be saved.

I'll never forget one summer weekend in the middle of July, just a few months after my 21st birthday. God was making me realize that all of the good things I had been doing – really good things like reading my Bible and praying – I was doing them not because I loved God but because I was trying to impress Him. Most of that weekend I was really sad because I was coming to realize how selfish and self righteous I was on the inside – in my heart where no one except God can see.

It wasn't until late Sunday afternoon as I was walking in the woods that God took away the blindness in my heart. Suddenly it hit me that Jesus is God the Son, that Jesus obeyed God perfectly like I never did and that Jesus died in my place. I finally admitted that I could not be saved by any of the good things I did, but that I could only be saved by trusting Jesus as my Lord. And that's what happened that afternoon: I stopped trying to do good so that God would like me, and I simply trusted that Jesus died for me—Jesus died for all the bad things I had thought and done, and Jesus died for all the good things I did while proudly trying to impress God.

Since that summer afternoon, my life has not been easy, but it has never been the same. I've loved trusting Jesus as God's one and only way of salvation, I've been delighted that Jesus is my Lord and my God, and I've been satisfied that Jesus is all I could need and could ever want in life.

Three months after God saved me, I went to college. Going to college ended in a very sad way, but I'll tell you about that next time.

Chapter 2
College Experience

Hello, again! My name is David Brainerd. The last time we were together I told you about some very sad times in my childhood. Can you remember the two really sad times I shared with you?

After I told you about those sad times, I told you how, when I was 21, God showed me that I could not be saved by all the good things I was doing. God changed my attitude about Him, and He led me to trust in Jesus alone to forgive me of my sin and save me from going to hell. God made me see that Jesus is God, Jesus is perfect, and Jesus died for my sins. What a happy day! I'll never forget it.

Three months after I trusted Jesus, I traveled 40 miles south to attend Yale College, one of the best schools in New England at that time. Yale was a Christian college, and I went there so that I could study to be a pastor. Because Yale was a school that taught the Bible, I thought that it would encourage me to become a stronger Christian, but I was wrong. I found that many of the students at Yale didn't really care about living for God – even though many of them were training to be pastors. I went to Yale for two years, then I got expelled – kicked out. Getting kicked out of Yale was the most embarrassing thing that had ever happened to me, and the year after I was expelled was the most depressing year of my life. Let me tell you what I did and how God used such a sad event to lead me.

I was 21 when I went to Yale College. That means I was one of the oldest students there. Most of the men who were in my class were younger than me. Even though they were younger than me, the upperclassmen treated me like their slave. That wasn't the only thing that was hard about Yale. My classes were really difficult: if I wanted to get good grades, I had to study really hard. And so I did. That meant I didn't get very good sleep. And because I didn't get enough sleep, I was often sick during college. In fact, four months into my first year, I had to leave Yale because I was so sick, and it took over a month at home before I healed.

Other things about college bothered me even more. It really bothered me that I had so little time to read my Bible and pray. It also bothered me that I wasn't allowed to go to churches where the gospel was being powerfully preached by traveling evangelists. Even though I wasn't allowed to go to those churches, I broke the rules and went anyway.

I would sneak out of my room and off the college property to go to those church meetings. I loved them because the Bible was really preached, not by some boring speaker who was trying to show off how smart he was. The Bible was preached by men who strongly believed what they said—by men who spoke with lots of enthusiasm. The preachers at those gatherings would boldly tell people that they were not good people but that they were sinners and that neither baptism nor church attendance would make God happy with them. They said that sinners needed to personally turn from their rebellion and personally trust in Jesus in order for their sins to be forgiven. They preached the good, hard truth. But the college didn't let the students attend those wonderful services. They were off limits.

You see, the college was filled with students and teachers who studied God's Word and liked to write out beautiful prayers to God and sermons about God, but many of them didn't have a personal relationship with God. A famous gospel preacher named George Whitefield came to preach at our college. He said, "It's possible that many of the pastors in our churches and teachers in our school might not be true Christians." The college leaders didn't like that at all. So immediately after that, they made a rule that students were never allowed to say that their teachers were not Christians. Rules like that really bothered me!

One day I went to chapel and heard one of my professors named Mr. Whittelsey (pronounced WHITTLE-zee; rhymes with "little z") pray. His prayer was one of those really long prayers with lots of big, beautiful words. But I didn't think that Professor Whittelsey actually meant anything he prayed; I didn't think he was a true Christian.

Later that day, a few friends and I were having a private conversation in one of the rooms at school. One of them asked me what I thought of Professor Whittelsey's long prayer in chapel. I immediately criticized it. I said, "This chair I'm leaning on has experienced more of God's salvation than Mr. Whittelsey has!" It was a very foolish thing for me to say, and I have wished a thousand times that I never said it, but I did.

Unknown to us, another student was listening in on our conversation and before long someone told the college dean. The dean called me to his office and asked if I had criticized Mr. Whittelsey. I told him that I had said it privately to a few friends, that I was wrong, and that I'd go back and apologize to them. The principal demanded that I apologize before the whole school. I told him that I would not publicly apologize for a private sin, and he expelled me.

The year after I was expelled from Yale was the worst of my life. I was so embarrassed that I had been expelled. Worse yet, it meant that I could never be a pastor! (In those days pastors had to be approved by a college like Yale.) I would have never recovered without good friends. God gave me a few pastors who knew what had happened to me at Yale. These men gave me so much support.

For the few months after I was expelled, Jedidiah Mills, a pastor who lived in Ripton (just ten miles from Yale), invited me to stay in his home, and Mr. Mills even helped me to keep studying. He also invited me to preach many times to his church and encouraged other pastors to invite me to speak in their churches. Best of all, Mr. Mills helped me to see that God was humbling me. It wasn't until I was expelled from Yale that I realized how smart I thought I was and how quick I was to harshly criticize others around me.

A few months after my expulsion, a few of these supportive pastors suggested that I give my life to preaching the gospel to the Indians—to live in Indian villages, to learn the Indian languages, to speak to the Indians the message about Jesus's death and resurrection, and to pray that God would establish churches among the Indians. I started praying about their suggestion, and as I prayed to God for direction, He gave me a burden to go to the Indians. God also kept showing me that I was a good-for-nothing sinner and that I was unworthy to be a missionary. So, with this growing sense of my own sin and with this growing burden to bring the gospel to the Indians, I took the encouragement of my friends and decided to give my life as a missionary to the Indians. That's something I would have never considered if I hadn't been expelled from college. You see, although it was really sad to get kicked out of college, God used it to humble me and to lead me to go to the Indians. (Throughout this year after his expulsion, David's most frequent sermons were based on Deuteronomy 8:2, "Remember how the Lord led you through the wilderness to humble you and teach you obedience.")

Chapter 3
Ministry to the Indians

The first time I talked with you I told you about two very sad times in my childhood. Can you remember them?

The next time I talked with you I told you about my sad experience at college. Can one of you remember what happened to me at college that made me so sad?

Now I'm going to tell you what my first two years as a missionary were like. Right from the start, I have to let you know that those first two years were sad ones. But before I tell you about them, I want you to take a minute to think about being sad. After hearing all that I've told you about me, some of you probably think that I was too sad. You're right; I was too sad. You might wonder why I wasn't happier, especially if I was a Christian. But I want you to know that following Jesus is both really happy and really sad. As a Christian, I'm happy whenever I remember that God has forgiven me of all my sin. I'm happy whenever I remember that Jesus is my Shepherd. I'm happy whenever I

remember that I'm going to live forever with Jesus and after I see Him, I'll never sin again. I can always be happy, can't I? But as a Christian I'm also sad much of the time. That's because there are so many people who don't trust Jesus and don't want to. There are so many churches that are struggling and so many Christians who are suffering. Another reason I'm always sad is that, until I see Jesus, I'm going to keep fighting with the sinful desires inside my heart.

See, I've come to learn that it's pretty normal for Christians to be both happy and sad at the same time. We're always happy that we know Jesus, and we're always sad that we don't love Him perfectly as we should. We're always thankful for the people who are being saved, and we're always sad for the people who don't want to be saved. Being a Christian is not easy! Don't believe it if people tell you that those who follow Jesus are always happy. It's not true.

The first missionary was the apostle Paul, who wrote many of the letters in the New Testament while he spread the gospel message throughout the Roman empire. During his missionary travels he was always experiencing conflict. He was a much better missionary than I was. He said that he was "always distressed, but never in complete despair." At one point, Paul even admitted that his burdens got so heavy that he "despaired of life itself" (2 Corinthians 4:8; 1:8). So the same man who "rejoiced in the Lord always" and "gave thanks in all circumstances" also experienced constant burdens that pressed heavily on his heart. Following Jesus is hard. But following Jesus is delightful, trusting Jesus is sweet, and knowing Jesus is wonderful. I want you to know that if I could live a thousand times, I'd choose to follow Jesus every time! (David actually said on his deathbed: "Had I a thousand souls, if they were worth anything, I would give them all to God.")

Now let me tell you about my first two years as a missionary. The same month I turned 25- years old (April 1743), I was sent to Stockbridge, Massachusetts, to learn how to live among the Indians. I learned from a well-known missionary named John Sergeant who had been preaching the gospel to the Indians for six years. (You can still visit the Mission House in Stockbridge. That house was built in 1742, and I spent a night there.) After spending a little time with Mr. Sergeant, he sent me out on my own.

I traveled 20 miles away to Kaunaumeek [pronounced CON-uh-meek], where Indians were settled at a split in Kinderhook Creek. For over a year I lived there among the Indians. Most people who wanted to preach to the Indians didn't actually live with them. Many were afraid to live with them. So missionaries would usually live nearby with other white people and traveled each day to and from the Indian village. I thought it was really important to live among them. But living with them made my life much more difficult. I couldn't understand their language (even though I was trying very hard to learn it), and anytime I talked with someone I had to talk through an interpreter. I had no friends and when you can't talk to people, there was no easy way for me to make friends. Although I constantly shared the good news about Jesus with the Indians at Kaunaumeek, I didn't see even one Indian trust Jesus as Saviour. That made me sad.

After that year, my leadership team encouraged me to move to Pennsylvania and work among the Indians who lived at "The Forks of the Delaware" River (Easton, Pennsylvania). I went there and did the same thing that I had done at Kaunaumeek: I prayed a lot, built a small cabin among the Indians, preached the Bible to groups of Indians, and then spent time in personal conversations with Indians to find out what they thought of the message I had preached. Of course, all of that talking was through an interpreter.

During that year at "The Forks" I made occasional trips to share the gospel with the Indians who lived at the split of the Susquehanna River (Sunbury, Pennsylvania). That large settlement was 100 miles away, and some of those long trips were treacherous. I remember one time I got lost in the middle of the Pennsylvania forest, and was afraid that I'd never make it out. I remember another time that my horse broke her leg, and it made me so sad when she died.

During another trip I got caught in the middle of an awful storm and I couldn't find any place to stop. I was so sick and wet and cold that I would've died that night if God hadn't directed me to a little house in the middle of nowhere. The family who lived there welcomed me into their warm home, gave me food and let me spend the night with them. These were some of the challenges I faced as I tried to share the gospel with the Indians in Pennsylvania.

Throughout that year in Pennsylvania, there were many times when it looked like God was working in the hearts of the Indians as they heard me preach the gospel, but none of them were willing to personally trust Jesus. After my fruitless year at Kaunaumeek, I worked another whole year and again saw no fruit. To work so hard at sharing the gospel and yet see no one trust Jesus crushed my heart. That's why I say that my first two years of work as a missionary were so sad. (Brainerd wrote that the reality of no fruit after two years "damped my spirits and was not a little discouraging.")

Missionary work is like that. There are many times that you keep on sharing the gospel even though no one is responding. You're like a farmer who keeps planting seeds and watering his fields, even though he doesn't see any plants growing. Even though it looks like nothing is happening, you just believe that God is going to use His word to change the lives of those who hear it, and you just keep sharing it.

Chapter 4
The Sweetest Year

This is now our fourth time together, and most of what I've told you till now has been sad. I've told you about my sad childhood, my sad experience at college, and about how sad I was after I had been with the Indians for two years and not even one Indian had claimed to trust Jesus. But what I'm going to tell you today is not sad.

While I was in Pennsylvania I traveled back and forth to another Indian settlement in New Jersey, Crossweeksung [pronounced cross-WEEK-sung], and, after my time in Pennsylvania, I moved to New Jersey to work among the Indians there. What happened during that year was nothing less than miraculous!

When I arrived at Crossweeksung, I didn't change anything I did. I prayed a lot for the Indians to trust Jesus. I lived among them. I frequently gathered them together for public preaching of the Bible. After I preached, I would invite individuals to have personal conversations about what they were hearing. But even though I didn't change what I was doing, God started showing His life-changing power in ways I had never seen before.

Here's how it all started. Just a month after I arrived in New Jersey, I went back to Pennsylvania for a two-week follow up visit. While there I baptized Moses Tautamy [pronounced TOT-uh-me] and his wife. Let me take a minute to tell you his story. Before I arrived, each of them had made the decision to trust Jesus for salvation. These were the first two Indians that I baptized; it happened two and a half years after my missionary work started. Tautamy was an Indian man about fifty years old. He had been my interpreter for the past year in Pennsylvania. When I first met him, he seemed to think that Christianity was a good way of life (he had been a hard alcoholic), but he didn't realize that he personally needed to be saved. About a month after I met Tautamy, God gave me a few opportunities to talk personally with him about his salvation, but it didn't seem to make any difference.

Later that fall Tautamy became very sick, and God used that time of sickness to show him that he wasn't ready to die. After a few weeks of being sick, God healed his body, but Tautamy's burden to be saved didn't go away. At one point he told me that trying to earn his salvation was like trying to climb an impossibly high mountain. God was showing him that he was a sinner who couldn't do anything to save himself. As God showed Tautamy how bad a sinner he was, God also showed Tautamy that there was hope in Jesus Christ—that God saves sinners by grace alone, not by any good works. Grace is a gift; it's not something you earn but something you're given even though you don't deserve it. Tautamy understood that salvation was a gift. After he told me about his personal trust in Jesus, I waited for six months to baptize Tautamy, and during that time I became convinced that he really understood the gospel and God had truly changed him.

Not only had God powerfully saved my interpreter, but God saved Tautamy so that he could be a powerful one. I think after his own salvation Tautamy's interpretations of my messages became more effective. When Tautamy and his wife were baptized, that was like a spark that ignited a fire that burned for a year. Throughout that year in New Jersey, I saw God save more than 100 Indians. I remember at least 12 baptism services that year. At one of those services in late August, I had the privilege of baptizing 15 adult Indians who had personally trusted Jesus and been reconciled to God. Just nine months after Tautamy and his wife were baptized, God had brought together a church of 130 Indians in New Jersey. It's just incredible what God did!

Sometimes people think that I just scared the Indians into trusting Jesus. When they hear that so many Indians became Christians, they imagine that I scared them with lots of messages about God's judgment and the horrors of hell. But that's not what actually happened. I didn't preach messages that focused on punishment; all my sermons focused on God's love and on His willingness to save sinners. I saw over 100 Indians trust Jesus, not because they were scared of punishment, but because they were convinced that Jesus loved them so much that He died for them. The Indians were convinced that they could be forgiven and accepted into God's family only if they trusted that Jesus's death and resurrection was for them and if they committed themselves to follow Him. The Indians were amazed that God would be so kind to rescue sinners like them and that God would welcome them into Heaven. There in New Jersey, I kept emphasizing the riches of God's kindness and patience, and, like Paul said (Romans 2:4), it led many Indians to repentance— to turn from their sins and trust Jesus to be their Saviour. (This paragraph simplifies and updates the language of David's own explanation in his journal comments after November 4, 1745.)

Throughout all of my missionary work among the Indians, I kept a daily journal of what I was doing and what was happening, and every couple of months I would send my most recent journals to my leadership team to make them aware of all that was happening. When I sent these reports of the amazing things that God was doing among the Indians in New Jersey, my mission board decided to publish my journals in a book. They thought that many other people throughout the world might be encouraged to hear what God was doing. In 1746 my mission board (The Society in Scotland for the Propagation of Christian Knowledge) published my journals in a book titled *The Marvels of God among the Indians*. (The title was actually Latin with a very long subtitle: *Mirabilia Dei inter Indio*, or *The Rise and Progress of a Remarkable Work of Grace amongst a Number of the Indians*.) Many people throughout the world heard about the marvelous things God was doing.

What a happy year that was! But, sadly, I wasn't able to stay in New Jersey. That's because I started to get very sick and had to leave New Jersey to get medical help.

Chapter 5
Death and Legacy

Hello! My name is Jonathan Edwards. I know you were probably expecting David Brainerd again. I know David's been telling you about his life, and you were probably expecting him to tell you the last part of his story, but I'm going to be the one who tells you how his life ended.

I met David for the first time a few years after he was expelled from college. I was 15 years older than David and had graduated from Yale College. In 1743 I was asked to speak at commencement, and I tried to help David get back in the school so he could finish his degree. But at that point David was already evangelizing the Indians, and he didn't want to stop doing that to go back to college.

A few years later I read David's descriptions of all the Indians in New Jersey who were trusting Jesus. I was so encouraged by what I read that I told my congregation all about it. (See Edwards's sermon, "Into the Highways and Hedges," April 1746.)

Throughout that year in New Jersey, even as God was saving more and more Indians, David was getting more and more sick. Even though God was clearly blessing David's preaching, David was finally forced to leave New Jersey and return to his home in New England so that he could get rest and recuperate.

My wife Sarah and I heard that the doctors had diagnosed David with a lung disease called tuberculosis and we knew that the doctors told David that he would not heal. Sarah and I agreed that we would offer to care for David in our home in Massachusetts, and David accepted our offer. He arrived on our doorstep in May 1747, just one month after he turned 29.

I asked Jerusha, my 17-year-old daughter, to be David's around-the-clock nurse, and she was glad to care for him. My family and I weren't bothered to have a sick man staying in our home who desperately needed our help. Actually, we all considered it an immense privilege God gave us: to provide care for a faithful Christian like David.

Unfortunately, from the time that David arrived at our house in May, he never got better, only worse. Yet as he suffered, David kept praying that God would be honored, whether he lived or died. At one point, when his pain was very, very bad, David prayed to God: "All my heart wants is to please You forever, to give You all I am, to be wholly devoted to glorifying You, Lord. That's the only way I'll be happy. God. All I want is to love and please and glorify You."

Throughout the four months he lived with us, I kept a record of David's weakening condition in my diary. I recorded on August 16th that David attended his last Sunday worship service. Two days later was the last day that David ever prayed with our family. And, let me tell you, we loved praying with David. He prayed very fervently for every member of my family while he was with us. About a week later (on Friday, August 28), was the last time that David ever went up a flight of stairs. A week after that is the last time he ever walked outside my house. Two weeks after that (on September 17) is the last time that David ever left his room. That weekend a few young people came to visit David. While they gathered at his bedside, he told them that they needed to prepare for death and that the most important way to prepare for death is to know for certain that God has given them a new heart through faith in Jesus. That was the last sermon I ever heard David preach. A week later (on Tuesday evening, September 29) was the last time David was able to get up from his bed. About a week later, I sat with a few others next to his bed as David slowly passed away. Here's what I wrote:

Elizabeth
Kerwoodwhittelsey
Died July 21st 1703
Aged 3 Years
As a tribute to the
memory of a
Beloved child
This Memorial is erected
by her Parents

Sacred to the
memory of the
Rev. David Brainard.
A faithful and laborious
Missionary to the
Stockbridge, Delaware,
and Susquehannah
Tribes of Indians,
who died in this town.
Oct. 10, 1747,
Æ. 32.

Pheobe
Kin Oc
170

Andrew Inglis
Clark
Judge, Husband, Father
Born 9 Dec 1600
Died 14 Oct. 1684
And
Grace Clark
His Wife
Born 27 June 1607
Died 25 June 1688

In the middle of the night, David's pain seemed to get worse than ever before. He told all of us that dying is a lot more painful than people imagine. Just before the sun came up, David's eyes stopped moving, his body stopped moving, and then he stopped breathing about 6 am, Friday, October 9, 1747. We are right to believe that as soon as David died, his soul was received by the Lord Jesus whom David dearly loved, and at that very moment, David was made perfect – what he so often and so passionately desired.

A few days after David died, I preached at his funeral on the wonderful truth that whenever a true believer leaves his body, he is immediately at home with the Lord. I'm sad to tell you that just a few months later I also preached the funeral for my own daughter Jerusha who had been David's nurse. We think that as she cared for David, she contracted the same disease that he had. But even though we lost our dear Jerusha, we would care for David again if God gave us the opportunity.

After David's death I read through all of his diaries. I was impressed by his Christian example, and I began to write a book about his life. That book was published about a year later, simply titled, *The Life of David Brainerd*. Among the dozens of books that I published throughout my life, this one has been the most popular.

If you read very much about my dear friend David Brainerd today, you'll see that most historians think that David didn't end up doing very much. You know, in a sense they're right. David was a missionary for only four years, he planted a church of about a hundred new believers, and you wouldn't have been able to find that church of Indians 30 years later. That's because the Indian population died out because of various diseases, because the New Englanders went to war with them, and because the white politicians kept forcing the Indians to move westward.

But God used David to do a lot! God used David to rescue over one hundred Indians from eternal hell. And God used the book I wrote about David to send missionaries all over the world. Other than the Bible, it's been one of the most influential books for missions ever written in the English language.

But notwithstanding all these imperfections, I am persuaded every pious and judicious reader will acknowledge, that what is here set before him is indeed a remarkable instance of true and eminent Christian piety in heart and practice — tending greatly to confirm the reality of vital ⁀⁀n, and the power of godliness — that it is ⁀⁀worthy of imitation, and many ways ⁀⁀cular⁀ ⁀s promote the spiritual benefit of the ⁀⁀car⁀ ⁀ver.

David Brainerd.

Through that book God used David Brainerd to encourage John Wesley as he trained hundreds of pastors. God used David's life to encourage William Carey to take the gospel to India. God used David to encourage A. J. Gordon as he led the Student Volunteer missionaries. And, among many others, God used David to encourage Jim Elliot to take the gospel to the Auca Indians in Ecuador at the cost of Jim's own life. It seems that, although God used David while he was alive, God used him even more powerfully after he died. (This statement is based on William Sweet: "David Brainerd dead was a more [powerful] influence for Indian missions and the missionary cause in general than was David Brainerd alive.")

God really used David to spread the gospel. God took a weak man like David, who was often sad and discouraged, who never graduated from college, and who didn't even live to be 30, and used him to save more than a hundred Indians and to encourage thousands of other missionaries to spread the message about how Jesus alone can save sinners. God loves to work like that. God loves to use weak things to show off how strong He is.

∽—∾

New York

Pennsylvania

Kaunameek

Kinderhook Creek

Northampton

Stockbridge

Massachusetts

Boston

Connecticut River

Connecticut

New
Haven

Haddam

Rhode
Island

Hudson River

Ripton

Yale
College

Montauk

Sunbury

Shamokin

Easton

New
Jersey

New York City

Crossweeksung

Philadelphia

Susquehanna River

– 65 –

But we have this treasure in earthen vessels, that the excellency of the power may be of God, and not of us.

2 Corinthians 4:7

Chapter 1

1. Where did David Brainerd grow up? What country was in charge of the colonies at that time? *(Connecticut colony; England)*
2. What was the first sad thing that David told us about? *(His parents both died when he was a child.)*
3. What was the second sad thing that David told us about? *(David didn't really like the God he was learning about; he thought God was unfair.)*
4. What was the happy thing that David told us about? *(He finally understood what trusting in Jesus meant.)*
5. Understand the Meaning: David told us that as he grew older, he realized that God was God. What did he mean by that? *(God is in control of everything, even when life is hard.)*
6. Understand the Meaning: Does everyone understand the good news about Jesus the very first time they hear it? *(No)* How old was David when he finally understood what salvation was? *(21 years old)*

Chapter 2

1. Where did David go to college? *(Yale University)*
2. What happened to David after being at college for two years? *(He was expelled.)*
3. Why did David get kicked out of college? *(He criticized a professor's boring prayer; he wouldn't apologize in public for something he had said privately to a friend.)*
4. Where did David's pastor-friends tell him to go as a missionary? *(To the native American Indians)*
5. Understand the Meaning: God used David's expulsion from college to help David. How did getting kicked out of college help David? *(It humbled him so he wasn't so proud and critical of others.)*

Chapter 3

1. Is living for Jesus (being a Christian) always going to be a happy time? *(No)*
2. David told us about someone from the Bible who was a missionary. What was his name and was his life always easy? *(The apostle Paul; no, his life was also hard)*
3. In today's story, how many years did David preach to the Indians without one person choosing to become a Christian? *(Two years)*
4. Understand the Meaning: Is God good? *(Yes)* Is God good even when things seem to be going badly? *(Yes: being*

sad is not a sin. Not believing God in despair is definitely wrong. Sad things happened to David Brainerd, but he kept believing that God is good.)
5. Understand the Meaning: Just because life is difficult and sad sometimes, does that mean that following Jesus is not worth it? Why? *(No; Christians have the joy of knowing God and living life with Him; God helps us understand life's joy and sadness. That's right. A difficult life lived as a Christian is better than an easy life lived without God.)*

Chapter 4

1. Where did David Brainerd go after he left Pennsylvania? *(New Jersey)*
2. Good things began to happen in New Jersey, but was David doing anything differently than he had in Pennsylvania? *(No, he was still praying a lot for people to trust Jesus and preaching the same way.)*
3. Who was the Indian man who became a true Christian? *(Tautamy, his translator. He realized that being saved from his sin was a gift, not something he had to work for!)*
4. At the end of one year, how many Indians were in the church David started in New Jersey? *(130)*
5. What did Tautamy say working hard for his salvation was like? *(Climbing an impossibly high mountain)*

Chapter 5

1. Who told us the rest of David Brainerd's story today? *(Jonathan Edwards)*
2. What did Jonathan Edwards think of David Brainerd? *(Jonathan admired David's faith in God and enjoyed their friendship.)*
3. What did David write in every day he was living with the Indians? *(A journal telling about everything that happened)*
4. After David died, what did Jonathan Edwards do to tell people about David's life? *(Wrote a book that has encouraged missionaries for the last 300 years)*
5. Understand the Meaning: How do we know that David Brainerd's life was not wasted? Or too short? *(God used everything that happened in his 29 years of life to save sinners, encourage countless missionaries, and help people see God's character more clearly.)*
6. Understand the Meaning: What do you find encouraging about David Brainerd's story? *(Allow a variety of answers)*

www.ingramcontent.com/pod-product-compliance
Lightning Source LLC
Chambersburg PA
CBHW042016080426
42735CB00002B/71